The First Christmas

ACCORDING TO LUKE

But thou, Bethlehem Ephratah, though thou be little among the thousands of Judah, yet out of thee shall he come forth unto me that is to be ruler in Israel; whose goings forth have been from of old, from everlasting.

Micah 5:2

This story of the birth of Jesus the Savior is presented

To _____

By _____

For _____

Date _____

———•◆•———

For unto us a child is born, unto us a son is given: and the government shall be upon his shoulder: and his name shall be called Wonderful, Counsellor, The mighty God, The everlasting Father, The Prince of Peace.

Of the increase of his government and peace there shall be no end, upon the throne of David, and upon his kingdom, to order it, and to establish it with judgment and with justice from henceforth even for ever. The zeal of the Lord of hosts will perform this.

Isaiah 9:6–7

The First Christmas

According to Luke the Evangelist

The Lord himself shall give you a sign; Behold,
a virgin shall conceive, and bear a son, and shall
call his name Immanuel.

Isaiah 7:14

CPH
SAINT LOUIS

orasmuch as many have taken in hand to set forth in order a declaration of those things which are most surely believed among us, even as they delivered them unto us, which from the beginning were eyewitnesses, and ministers of the word; it seemed good to me also, having had perfect understanding of all things from the very first, to write unto thee in order, most excellent Theophilus, that thou mightest know the certainty of those things, wherein thou hast been instructed.

Luke 1:1–4

In the days of Herod, the king of Judaea . . . the angel Gabriel was sent from God unto a city of Galilee, named Nazareth, to a virgin espoused to a man whose name was Joseph, of the house of David; and the virgin's name was Mary.

nd the angel came in unto her, and said, Hail, thou that art highly favoured, the Lord is with thee: blessed art thou among women.

And when she saw him, she was troubled at his saying, and cast in her mind what manner of salutation this should be.

And the angel said unto her, Fear not, Mary: for thou hast found favour with God.

And, behold, thou shalt conceive in thy womb, and bring forth a son, and shalt call his name JESUS.

He shall be great, and shall be called the Son of the Highest: and the Lord God shall give unto him the throne of his father David:

And he shall reign over the house of Jacob for ever: and of his kingdom there shall be no end.

hen said Mary unto the angel, How shall this be, seeing I know not a man?

And the angel answered and said unto her, The Holy Ghost shall come upon thee, and the power of the Highest shall over-shadow thee: therefore also that holy thing which shall be born of thee shall be called the Son of God.

And, behold, thy cousin Elisabeth, she hath also conceived a son in her old age: and this is the sixth month with her, who was called barren.

For with God nothing shall be impossible.

And Mary said, Behold the handmaid of the Lord; be it unto me according to thy word. And the angel departed from her.

nd it came to pass in those days, that there went out a decree from Caesar Augustus, that all the world should be taxed.

(And this taxing was first made when Cyrenius was governor of Syria.)

nd all went to be taxed, every one into his own city.

nd Joseph also went up from Galilee, out of the city of Nazareth, into Judaea,

unto the city of David, which is called Bethlehem; (because he was of the house and lineage of David:)

To be taxed with Mary his espoused wife, being great with child.

And so it was, that, while they were there, the days were accomplished that she should be delivered.

nd she brought forth her firstborn son, and wrapped him in swaddling clothes, and laid him in a manger; because there was no room for them in the inn.

nd there were in the same country shepherds abiding in the field, keeping watch over their flock by night.

nd, lo, the angel of the Lord came upon them, and the glory of the Lord shone round about them: and they were sore afraid.

And the angel said unto them, Fear not: for, behold, I bring you good tidings of great joy, which shall be to all people.

For unto you is born this day in the city of David a Saviour, which is Christ the Lord.

And this shall be a sign unto you; Ye shall find the babe wrapped in swaddling clothes, lying in a manger.

And suddenly there was with the angel a multitude of the heavenly host praising God, and saying,

Glory to God in the highest, and on earth peace, good will toward men.

nd it came to pass, as the angels were gone away from them into heaven, the shepherds said one to another, Let us now go even unto Bethlehem, and see this thing which is come to pass, which the Lord hath made known unto us.

nd they came with haste, and found Mary, and Joseph, and the babe lying in a manger.

And when they had seen it, they made known abroad the saying which was told them concerning this child.

And all they that heard it wondered at those things which were told them by the shepherds.

ut Mary kept all these things, and pondered them in her heart.

✸

And the shepherds returned, glorifying and praising God for all the things that they had heard and seen, as it was told unto them.

And the child grew, and waxed strong in spirit, filled
with wisdom: and the grace of God was upon him.

Luke 2:40

Edited by James Heine
Design by Karen Pauls and Ed Luhmann

The Scripture text in this publication is from the Authorized or King James Version of the Bible.

Concordia Publishing House (CPH) is the publishing arm of the The Lutheran Church—Missouri Synod, an international
church serving and being served by people in many nations. In an effort to be good stewards of its resources and to provide a
global witness to its mission and ministry, CPH will from time to time use the services of international companies in the
production of its products.

Copyright © 1993 Concordia Publishing House
3558 South Jefferson Avenue, St. Louis, MO 63118-3968
Manufactured in Mexico

5   6   7   8   9   10   02   01   00   99